W9-ANW-372

Firefighters
Help Us

Aaron R. Murray

Enslow Elementary
an imprint of

 Enslow Publishers, Inc.
40 Industrial Road
Box 398
Berkeley Heights, NJ 07922
USA

http://www.enslow.com

Enslow Elementary, an imprint of Enslow Publishers, Inc.
Enslow Elementary® is a registered trademark of Enslow Publishers, Inc.

Copyright © 2013 by Enslow Publishers, Inc.
All rights reserved.

No part of this book may be reproduced by any means
without the written permission of the publisher.

Library of Congress Cataloging-in-Publication Data

Murray, Aaron R.
  Firefighters help us / Aaron R. Murray.
     p. cm. — (All about community helpers)
  Includes index.
  Summary: "Introduces pre-readers to simple concepts about what firefighters do using short sentences
and repetition of words"—Provided by publisher.
  ISBN 978-0-7660-4047-2
  1. Fire fighters—Juvenile literature. 2. Rescue work—Juvenile literature. 3. Fire extinction—Juvenile
literature. I. Title.
  HD8039.F5M87 2013
  628.9'2023—dc23
                                            2011031046

Future editions:
Paperback ISBN 978-1-4644-0053-7
ePUB ISBN 978-1-4645-0960-5
PDF ISBN 978-1-4646-0960-2

Printed in the United States of America
032012 Lake Book Manufacturing, Inc., Melrose Park, IL
10 9 8 7 6 5 4 3 2 1

To Our Readers: We have done our best to make sure all Internet Addresses in this book were active
and appropriate when we went to press. However, the author and the publisher have no control over and
assume no liability for the material available on those Internet sites or on other Web sites they may link
to. Any comments or suggestions can be sent by e-mail to comments@enslow.com or to the address on
the back cover.

♻ Enslow Publishers, Inc., is committed to printing our books on recycled paper. The paper in every
book contains 10% to 30% post-consumer waste (PCW). The cover board on the outside of each book
contains 100% PCW. Our goal is to do our part to help young people and the environment too!

Photo Credits: © 2011 Photos.com, a division of Getty Images. All rights reserved, p. 8-9;
iStockphoto.com: © Daniel Bendjy, p. 1, © Jeremy Sterk, p. 16, © Michael Courtney, p. 22;
Shutterstock.com, pp. 3, 4, 6, 7, 10–11, 12–13, 14, 18–19, 20.

Cover Photo: © Daniel Bendjy/iStockphoto.com

Note to Parents and Teachers

Help pre-readers get a jumpstart on reading. These lively stories introduce simple concepts with
repetition of words and short simple sentences. Photos and illustrations fill the pages with color and
effectively enhance the text. Free Educator Guides are available for this series at www.enslow.com.
Search for the *All About Community Helpers* series name.

Contents

Words to Know

alarm   ladders

Firefighters train hard to put out fires.

Firefighters are always ready to help.

Their fire trucks are always ready to go.

The alarm goes off.

Rrrring! Rrrring!

Firefighters race
to help.

Firefighters spray water on the fire.

**Firefighters use
tall ladders.**

Firefighters go into burning buildings.

Firefighters put out forest fires.

Firefighters also help people who are hurt.

19

Firefighters
are brave.

Firefighters
save lives.

Do you like helping people?

You may want to be a firefighter.

Read More

Gorman, Jacqueline Laks. *Firefighters*. New York: Gareth Stevens Publishing, 2010.

Minden, Cecilia. *Firefighters*. North Mankato, Minn.: Child's World, 2006.

Vogel, Elizabeth. *A Day in the Life of a Firefighter*. New York: PowerKids Press, 2002.

Web Sites

National Fire Prevention Association. *Sparky the Fire Dog.*
<http://www.sparky.org/story.html>

U.S. Fire Administration. *For Kids.*
<http://www.usfa.dhs.gov/kids/flash.shtm>

Index

Guided Reading Level: C
Guided Reading Leveling System is based on the guidelines recommended by Fountas and Pinnell.
Word Count: 73